The Man and the Myth

<u>First Published 1986</u>

Mitchell Bunting was born in Glasgow. He studied at Mansfield College, Oxford, where he researched much of the material for this book as his history thesis. He was ordained into the ministry and inducted as the Associate Minister at Carrs Lane United Reformed Church, Birmingham, in October 1985.

A member of the Iona Community since 1982, particularly associated with work among young people as a clown with Christ's message of turning the world upside-down, he now lives with 6 others in a Columban House in Handsworth, Birmingham.

Cover Design by Laurie Carter from a concept by Brian and Anna

WILD GOOSE PUBLICATIONS

The wild goose is a Celtic symbol of the Holy Spirit. It serves as the logo of Iona Community Publications.

The Abbey, Isle of Iona, by Oban, Argyll. PA76 6SN

COLUMBA

The Man and the Myth

by Mitchell Bunting

INTRODUCTION

A Study of Columba encounters many difficulties. Information is vague; often contradictory and overlaid by centuries of myth making. His own people used mythology to explain things. This could be used to record events, reveal great truths and unfortunately to distort facts. Even up to the last century, writers continued to shroud Columba in romantic fantasy.

Now a realistic picture of Columba has emerged. Some scholars didn't like what they found as it seemed Columba was more a warrior than a monk. Recently the balance has been restored.

This study tries to make sense of the contradictions between angelic monk and tribal warrior by investigating the man and his people.

Columba was a Celt and it is here that any study of such a man must begin. The Celts had been on a westward wander for thousands of years and had scarcely come out of the iron age. Like the ancient Greeks they had an overall cultural identity but the different clans fought constantly. Columba's own race, the Scots, came from Spain around 100 B.C. where they met earlier migrators, the Cruithne, who had mixed with the local population and covered part of Northern Ireland. In Scotland, or Alba as it was then called, related races were the Britons and the Picts. Between these peoples, and even within their own tribes, were constant battles. It was not all treachery - some outstanding tales of courage and loyalty shine through to give credit.

In Ireland the basic political unit was the extended family, known as the TUATH, each with its protector or RI. There were around 150 such TUATHs in North Ireland, in 5 loose confederations, each with its own RI or king. Above them all, seated at Tara the ritual centre, was the ARDRI or high king (somewhat like the Old Testament kings) as a semi divine battle leader. The kings were all chosen as the best candidates from a system that was hereditary as well as elective. The three classes were the warriors and chiefs, the workers or serfs, and the bards or FILIDH. It was in this last class that were the learned Druids, (the philosophers, physicians and magicians) and the BRIEVES (the law makers and advisors). On major occasions the chief advisor was the OLAVE BRIEVE who was the king's advisor, since usually the king couldn't read.

The Celts were surrounded by taboos and omens - nature ruled every move they made. Their worship was a hotch-potch constructed to make sense of these omens. The coming of Christianity liberated the Celts from these restrictions, but the church continued much of the folklore.

Before Columba's time there had been a veritable dark age for a time, now a new light was shining in this remote fringe of Christendom. At Tara, a venerated holy place for thousands of years, the new age was dawning on the Ui Neills of Ireland. Newly Christian, they still continued their ancient ways. Every three years a festival of games, ritual and law making was held since the legendary Niall of Nine Hostages - the ancestor of the Ui Neills. Now in 560 A.D. Dairmaid macGebaill of the Southern Ui Neill held the feast.

The first recorded evangelism in Britain comes from Ninian, a Briton who, in 397 after returning from Rome via Tours, set up a monastery at Candida Casa (Whithorn) in Galloway in order to convert the Britons, who were Roman influenced, and even the Pictish pagans of southern Pictland. He had been taught by the famous Martin, who, as a disillusioned soldier, had become a monk influenced by St. Antony and, having been exiled by the Arian Bishop of Rome, eventually settled in Tours where he became bishop in 372.

Patrick as a youth was captured by the pagan Irish, escaped, trained at Whithorn then returned to bring the gospel to the Irish. He brought forgiveness to these warriors by the example of his own return. He founded a tribal church based on existing Celtic systems and totally unlike the Roman church which depended on large buildings and population centres. This was the church Columba grew up in. There is a Christian link from Martin to Ninian to Patrick who baptised Conal Gulban, Columba's great grandfather.

The Irish monks taught by example and countered the powerful and esoteric druids with love, firmness and openess. They preached the Gospel they had memorised and countered revenge with forgiveness. They were the Christian front line, an earthly colony of the Kingdom. Hence the name MILES CHRISTI, soldiers of Christ (This is the same name used today by members of the Iona Community). There were no martyrs in this period so great was the acceptance, but not necessarily the conversion, of the pagan Irish. They spread by establishing a site for worship and education, developing it, and then moving on in a systematic way. In many cases they took over existing pagan sites. The druids had taught - but mostly in a select way, now the monks taught freely to all who came supplying a place to live and all materials free of charge.

The Irish conversion was quick - just 150 years. Not all were converted totally and perhaps it was this tension that led so many monks to take white martyrdom and become peregrini - that is exiled pilgrims. A famous contemporary of Columba's was Columbanus who settled in Babbio, Italy!

Contemporary monks who travelled to Britain before and after Columba were Comgall of Bangor; Brendan who set up houses on Seil, Tiree and Bute by 545; Moluag who set up houses on Lismore, Skye and in Pictland at Rosemarkie; and Blaan who set up houses on Bute and at Dunblane. Main monasteries in his time were Candida Casa of the British church, the church of David in Wales, and Bangor and Clonard in Ireland.

The Roman church adapted nature by building large churches and worshipping with Ikons developed from pagan temples and idols. The Celtic church too developed its pagan roots. Instead of worshipping nature to avoid bad luck, they now worshipped nature as God's good creation. The liturgy was the Gallican liturgy of St. Martin and Easter was the main festival. The choir followed the style of the bards, and psalm singing was a main part of the worship, which was based on contemplation and penance.

Bishops in Ireland only had the privilege of ordination. At first there were few large buildings; perhaps they followed the pagan tradition of worshipping out-of-doors. Certainly they led an out-door life, travelling and farming. They carried their new methods of agriculture wherever they went.

This was no heretical sect, nor a freak of fringe Christendom - it was the family church of Ireland who took the Gospel literally and lived in an age of openness to miraculous events. They continued to live in a kind of dream world longing for the Kingdom and finding tastes of it in remote and wild places. If to know the Roman Church one must walk the sights of Rome, then to know the Celtic Church one must walk the islands.

EVIDENCE IN LITERATURE

The basic sources are the Annals of Ulster and Tigernach which record battles and important events; the hagiography by Adomnan the 9th Abbot of Iona; the references in Bede; the Old Irish Life; and the Amhra Columcille and other poems either written as devotions or by tradition by Columba himself.

Of all these, Adomnan's 'Life of St. Columba', written around 688, 100 years after Columba, is the most important. Adomnan did not write an historical book, rather a book to inspire the faith in his own time. Facts are left out as being either irrelevant or as being harmful to his purposes. It is the oldest complete biography after the Roman Period and the oldest surviving manuscript is the 'A Codex' taken to an Irish monastery in Austria, during Viking attacks, for protection. It is now in a Swiss museum. The writer is thought to have been Dorbene, a subsequent Abbot of Iona who died in 713. His name appears at the end of Codex A at a place where each copyist would place his own name. Other codexes, although of later date, are still valuable because of better spelling.

The book is in Latin and has three parts dealing with prophecies, miracles and visions. Adomnan's purpose for writing is stated in the opening sentence, "to respond to the importunity of the brothers". He had been involved in the 'Easter Controversy' by turning over to the Roman methods while visiting Jarrow in Northumbria. Upon returning to Iona the brothers felt he had betrayed Columba - it is to correct this that he sets out to show how blessed Columba was to the extent of proving he was an apostle as potent as Peter in miraculous gifts. He was writing for the survival of his community - it is no wonder he left out anything controversial. Although it is a spiritual book there are many clues which match with the Annals. The myths may seem unreal and frustrating but are for the most part symbolic stories. He wrote with material diligently assembled from the oral tradition and from the written work of an earlier Abbot Cuimmene and drew inspiration from the Bible and St. Antony. To assess its value we must be aware of the myth language of Columba's time and later, and the reasons for writing. His oft said phrase, "why say more?" is infuriating; we wish he had. However an outline of Columba comes out of these stories. His taking up a diet of nettle soup suggests solidarity with the poor. His turning foul water to pure speaks of the living water he preached. Likewise the sour fruit made sweet speaks of the new way of Christianity over pagan. The pagans lived by fear, Columba struck at the root of this fear by praising creation - for this he is credited with the hymn Altus. The story of him blessing a man's cows up to 105 and no more sounds crazy but reveals that the man had learnt from the monks to give extra away. In such farming stories do we get the most realistic picture.

There are three ways we can appreciate Columba's miraculous powers.

1) They are biblical parallels to prove his sanctity; for instance the resurrection incident and the changing of water into wine.

2) Columba's common sense, good humour, political insight and knowledge of weather; for instance the contrary winds and the healing of a nose bleed by pinching with the fingers.

3) Genuine miracles?

Columba was a man of faith living a literal Gospel. Our doubts speak more of us than of Columba. Adomnan would only record the (few?) successful healings - Columba's failures would be forgotten. For Adomnan the facts are irrelevant. The true fact is 'God is with Columba'. Colouring by successive storytellers also may have added to such tales.

The miracles in the Gospels are recorded as signs of proof of Jesus' identity; wonder working was shunned by Jesus himself yet the Celtic Church saw miracles as magical events. No wonder - the Celts were just out of the Iron Age and did not have 1500 years of Monotheism behind them.

Columba is seen to be more like Moses or Joshua but he did strive for an apostolic lifestyle. The extremes of Adomnan's description of Columba are balanced by the references to feast days and celebrations for guests. He has recorded deeds of symbolic value perhaps in an attempt also to clarify legends already established. Certainly through the ages these actions can speak to us louder than words.

Bede, a monk in Northumbria, lived between 673 - 735. In his book he records Columba and the Easter controversy. He tells of Columba converting the Northern Picts in 565 and confirms Columba's rank as presbyter rather than bishop and also confirms the house of Durrow. In the Easter controversy Bede supports the Iona monks' characters but disapproves of their date and their haircut shaved in the fashion of the druids rather than the crown to symbolise the thorns of Jesus.

The Old Irish Life was a homily composed around 1000 for use at the festival of St. Columba. A translation can be found in Skene's Celtic Scotland, Volume II and is based on the two manuscripts - the 'Leabar Breac' (1397) and the 'book of Lismore' (1460). There are many parallels with Adomnan. The extra parts can be explained by the writers' desire to show Columba as the perfect pilgrim in the style of Abraham. His contact with other saints and his accomplishments in church building and book copying add to his sanctity. The Columban Church was predominant in Scotland over the Pictish and British Churches, so it was good policy to give Columba all the credit.

EVIDENCE IN ART AND ARCHEOLOGY

In evidence of Columba's lifetime little is extant. However the advances made in the 8th Century suggest that in Columba's time things were developing. The illuminated book of Kells, which is of mixed influence, was started on Iona and removed during Viking raids to Kells. This shows how active the Columban Church was at this time. The book of Durrow is earlier and may contain Columba's writing. The Cathach however is more promising. It is believed to be the psalter that Columba copied from Finnian of Moville around 560. It was in good condition in medieval times when it was encased in silver, but when opened recently it contradicted Adomnan's claims to Columba's books being unable to be drowned (perhaps symbolic of baptism and true life). It has started to rot! The text is the Gallican Jerome psalter and the style is an Irish script fancier than plain Roman uncial showing an emotional involvement on the part of the copyist. This style was ancient and developed into the magnificent illuminated texts.

The Monymusk reliquary, which was carried into battle right until Bannockburn, is a small casket devoid of Christian symbolism suggesting an ancient date. It has beautiful pagan carving and was said to have contained relics of Columba.

The first settlements on Iona were on top of Dun Bhuig and were inhabited in the first centuries. There appears to have been no settlements on the East of Iona till Columba, though there were native peoples and Dalriad Scots on Mull and in Argyll. The burial ground was in use before Columba and remains in use today. The tale of Oran is found in the Old Irish Life and the name Relig Odhran is taken from him. The surviving burial stones are later than Columba. All Scottish kings up to Kenneth MacAlpine, including 'Macbeth' and 'Duncan' as well as Irish, French and Norse kings, are buried in this graveyard.

Many names on the island cannot be traced back beyond the 19th century. Some are ancient. Evidence suggests Columba's site was near the present Abbey. Tor Abb, a small hill to the East of the Abbey, has a small cell and a cross base on top. The cross base has places for wedges meaning a wooden cross, which suggests an ancient date. The cell when excavated had no finds in it. This suggests that it was preserved out of sanctity and the evidence of a wooden cross suggests it was a venerated site before the 7th century (stone was used thereafter). Together with Adomnan's reference to a daytime cell these facts point to the authenticity of this being Columba's actual cell! From there he could look out over the monastery and over the Sound of Iona to Mull. The well, just to the right of the cross below, may well be very ancient, and the small shrine, just to the rear of the cross, is the site where Columba was buried before his remains were taken to Ireland.

Four crosses remain, two complete; John's cross and Martin's cross. They date from the 8th Century. There are several cross bases and many are cut for wooden crosses which in Columba's time would have been a Chi-Rho shape perhaps. The stone called Columba's pillow, now in the museum, relates to Adomnan's account of Columba's austere sleeping habits. The incised ringed cross is later, since ringed crosses only started in the 7th or 8th centuries. The stone is unlikely to be authentic - if it is, Columba must have had a hard time.

Pictish monoliths of pagan symbolism only are to be found in greatest concentration in the North East of Scotland, supporting the theory of the Pictish capital near Inverness. Later Pictish slab stones of mixed Christian and pagan design are found most in the South of Scotland and have a strong Northumbrian influence, supporting the theory that the Picts were not converted until long after Columba.

Columban churches found all over Scotland are either a result of the Dalriadic swamping of the Pictish and British Churches in and after 850, or are later dedications or corruptions of names. Only churches called 'Columcille' or similar may be authentic foundations. Columba and Colum were popular names!

COLUMBA

Adomnan, dating by battles, gives Columba's year of birth as 521. The Old Irish Life is questionably more exact with Thursday the 21st December! His noble parentage is without question, although his mother's side may be a later fabrication. She, Ethne, is accredited to the royal blood of Leinster. His father, Felim macFergus, was of the Northern Ui Neill and a descendant of Niall of 9 hostages. His great grandfather had been a slave raider whose sons were converted by Patrick. Among them Cral Galban, King of Donegal. His father's mother was the daughter of Lorn macErc, the prince of Dalriada, who had been squeesed out by the Northern Ui Neill around 500 and had settled in Alba with his brothers Angus and Fergus, setting up capital at Dun Add.

Of his father's paternal line, he was of the Cenel Conaill of the Northern Ui Neill, based in Donegal, and on his father's maternal line he was related to the first Scots to settle in Alloa. Larn and Fergus were buried on Iona.

Later writers stress his aptness for kingship, but his parents either through insight or tithing, established him as a child in the church. Writers also stress his nativity - almost in a biblical way - in order to point out how great a man was this "Columba, favoured by God".

His parents sent him, in the Irish manner, to a foster father Cruithnechan, an Irish Pict. this was decisive - if he were to become a warrior, at this stage he would have been sent to train in martial arts. Instead he was taught to read by an old priest! He was baptised 'Crimthan' (the fox) by Cruithnechan, but later his name was changed to Columcille, which translated means dove of the church, as a result of his love of reading and worshipping. A more literal translation is 'pigeon of the cell'! The Old Irish Life mentions three stories at this stage. Firstly that he learned the alphabet by eating shaped biscuits, which is realistic; secondly that he, as a boy, remembered the 100th psalm when his aged master forgot, which is realistic in a church where the 150 psalms were repeated daily from memory; and thirdly a resurrection story no doubt influenced by the Bible.

Born rich, he chose poverty; born Royal he became a monk. He entered the monastery of Finnian of Moville as a student of scripture and became a deacon. Finnian trained at Candida Casa and was of Roman influence. It was here Columba aked for gifts of purity, wisdom and prophecy relating to body, mind and soul. He performed his first miracle (according to Adomnan) and changed water into wine for the eucharist. An event steeped in exciting symbolism!

His next teacher was Gemman, a Christian bard in Leinster (supporting his mother's heritage) who taught him preaching and Celtic heritage. Here he encountered sanctuary breaking for the first time. This story is parallel in a way to Peter striking down Ananias. It is more realistic to assume, after the attacker had killed the girl in front of Columba, that her friends, then or soon after, sought revenge. Columba may have cursed - it was his only weapon - but his concern for human rights must not be overlooked.

His fourth teacher is given in the Old Irish Life as Finnian of Clonard. Adomnan is not clear about his upbringing. It is not known for sure if there was one Finnian or two, due to spelling difficulties and descriptions of 'old age' and being a bishop. Keeping in mind the problem, most people follow the Irish Life. The story of Columba's hut built near the church that expanded, reflects Finnian of Clonard who, trained himself at the Welsh monasteries of Cadoc, Gildas and David, now trained as many as 3000 young monks! Finnian, who was an Irish Pict, sent him to be ordained by Bishop Echtan. That he was ordained presbyter and not bishop has caused later writers to invent stories explaining this. It may well be that Finnian, keeping his own bishop status secret, sought to keep monks presbyters, due to the corruption of British bishops he had heard of from Gildas.

He set out with his friends, known as the 12 apostles of Ireland, to join the monastery of Mobhi (flat face) at Glasnevin near Dublin. In 543-4 yellow plague swept through Europe and decimated the monks. The monastery was closed by Mobhi and Columba returned home to Derry. Mobhi died soon after and is recorded in the Annals. His dying words gave Columba permission to set up his own monastery. The Old Irish Life tells how his cousin, King Aid macAinmire gave him a royal grant of an oak grove. Derry means the place of oaks and had been a pagan holy place before Columba. The stories related to this are steeped in pagan myth. There is little to suggest he founded Derry except an entry from later in the Annals. He may well have started a small community here which grew into a full monastery. At this point the Old Irish Life claims he visited Rome and Tours. It seems this is based on a corruption of Torinis which in fact is Tory Island off Donegal.

His next settlement was at Durrow, which means the place of oaks and was again a previous pagan sanctuary, given to him by Aid son of Brendan. Adomnan suggests that Columba established Durrow much later in life and Bede confirms Durrow as a genuine Columban monastery. It could be that at this early stage Columba settled a small house, which he later turned into a full monastery. This also suggests that the Old Irish Life is suspect in accuracy. For certain Columba did found Durrow. A tale here tells how he turned bitter fruit into sweet - a tale symbolic of changing pagan things into Christian. Kells is another settlement only known through the Old Irish Life. Kells was a Columban house, but it may not have been founded by Columba but by one of his followers, even as late as the escape from the Vikings on Iona. If Columba did found these monasteries, then they were strategically placed in the Irish Kingdoms. He may well have helped in setting up churches and small communities in Ireland, but this is all uncertain.

CULDREMNE

Britain consisted of four main races. To the North the Picts, to whom Ninian and others had travelled; to the South and West the Britons, who were a mixture of pagans and Roman remnant Christians; to the South and East the thoroughly pagan Saxons; and the small nation of Scots living in Argyll who were Christian. After the fall of Rome the Saxons took much land and the British pagans ousted the Briton Christians causing Kentigern and Gildas to go to Wales. The war of the faiths raised pagan hopes even in Ireland. High King Diarmait of the Southern Ui Neill was partly a Christian but was wholly a pagan sympathiser. The popular stories of hereafter may well have been put out by the pagans as propaganda to discredit Columba who was a leading Christian and was of 'kingly material'.

At this time Columba made a copy of a psalter in the Jerome version entrusted to Finnian of Moville for safe keeping – not so much from Columba himself but from the risks of copying introducing mistakes. Tradition has it that the dispute was taken to the Ard Ri Diarmait whose judgement "to every cow its calf; to every book its copy" was against Columba. The judge at this occasion would have been the pagan Olave Brieve Bec macDe. Finnian and Columba appear to have overlooked Paul's instructions about Christian disputes, however the church at this time was totally immersed in secular affairs so the reciprocal could also be true.

In 560 Diarmaid held the Tara festival. It would have been here the appeal took place. During the festival games Curnan, son of King Aid of Connaught, killed a playmate in a hurley match and was subsequently killed by Diarmaid's men whilst in the protection of Columba. In the law of the land he should have been set free after paying the blood fine. Diarmaid had broken the law of the land and the church's rights.

The Annals of Tigernach may be trusted that this was the cause that led to the battle of Culdremne. National feelings would have been high at this time; it would have taken little to bring the clans into conflict. Yes this, and not a minor dispute between two monks no matter how angry they got. Nor was the

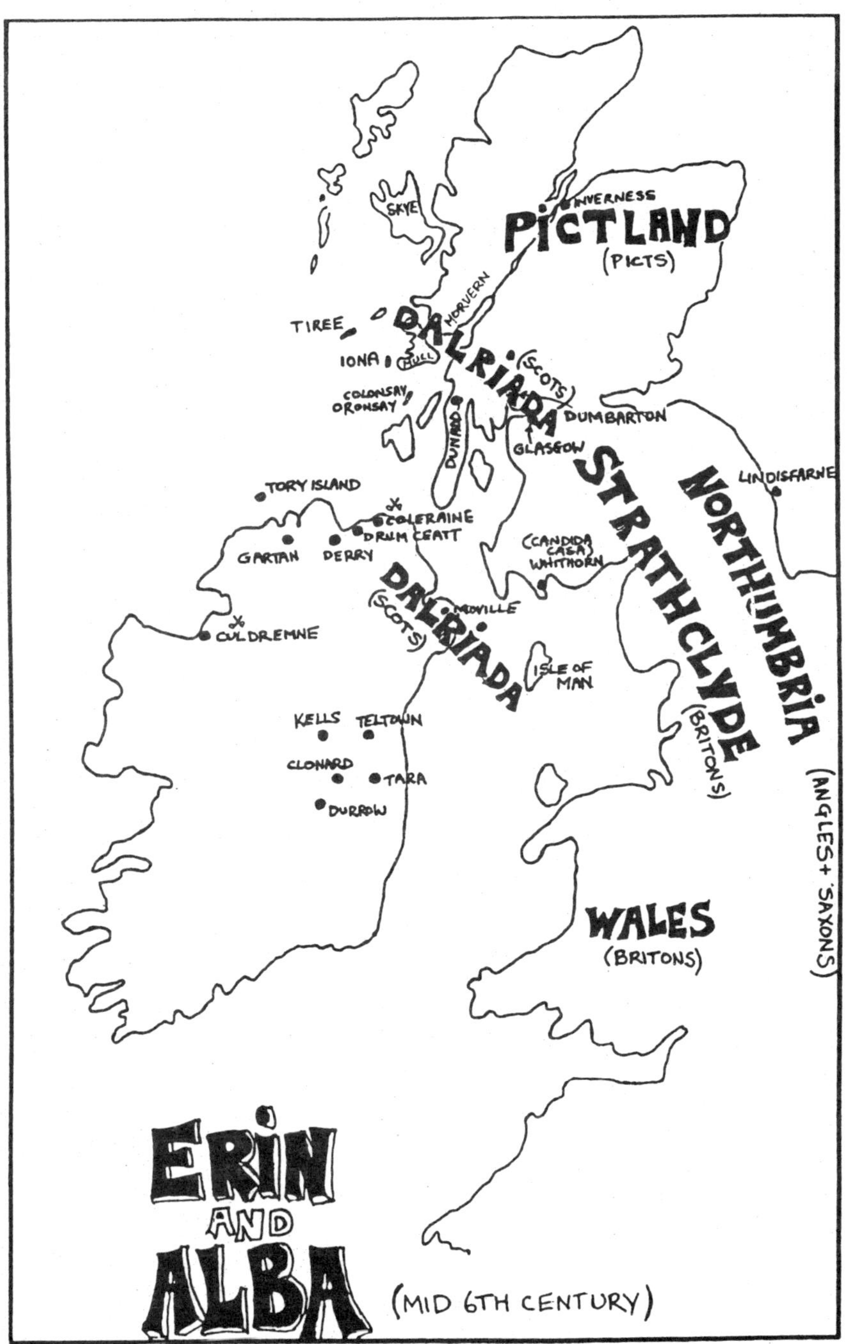

PICTLAND
(PICTS)
INVERNESS
SKYE
TIREE
DALRIADA
MORVERN
(SCOTS)
IONA
MULL
COLONSAY
ORONSAY
DUNADD
DUMBARTON
GLASGOW
STRATHCLYDE
(BRITONS)
NORTHUMBRIA
LINDISFARNE
TORY ISLAND
COLERAINE
DRUM CEATT
GARTAN
DERRY
(CANDIDA
CASA)
WHITHORN
DALRIADA
(SCOTS)
MOVILLE
CULDREMNE
ISLE OF
MAN
KELLS
TELTOWN
CLONARD
TARA
DURROW
(ANGLES + SAXONS)
WALES
(BRITONS)
ERIN
AND
ALBA
(MID 6TH CENTURY)

battle a fight purely for the faith for Diarmaid wasn't totally anti-Christian, neither were the Ui Neill totally Christian. This battle was a continuation of clan warfare with Columba, either by his choice or against his will, as the spiritual leader of the Northern Ui Neill. He was involved in the battle for he had a duty to pray for his people and for protection of his monasteries and houses. Later stories of Columba's involvement in the slaughter could be true - Celts were very easily angered, but it could also be that these stories were pagan propaganda in an attempt to split the Christian Church. Adomnan and the Old Irish Life say little and Adomnan may even be covering up when he mentions 'excusable offences'. The Annals of Ulster state that Columba prayed for his side to win. Presumably both sides would have used prayer and ritual as a psychological device.

The Ui Neill and the Cinel Conaill fought presumably to protect Columba's honour (having been disgraced by having his sanctuary broken) and the men of Connaught joined them in victory over Diarmaid's men in 561 at Culdremne. The 3000 lost against only one is surely a later gloss symbolistic of the Christian victory over the pagans.

After this the political power of the pagans led by the druids was broken and Tara ceased to be important till it was revived years later. Diarmaid was murdered by Black Aid, a suspicious monk whom Columba cursed. Both men died the mythical threefold way of piercing, burning and drowning.

Columba was not innocent, neither was he wholly responsible. His involvement must be seen in the light of his responsibility to his tribal church and his greater responsibility to pray for a Christian victory over the pagans. It is unlikely that he led the battle, his role was almost certainly as a non combatant. Critics of his behaviour would do well to study present church support for war as well.

<u>EXILE</u>

Tradition has it that after the battle Columba was excommunicated for his part, banished and told by his soul friend Laisren to win as many pagan souls as had been lost in the battle. This happened at the synod of Teltown near Tara. Adomnan tells us he was wrongly excommunicated and Brendan supported Columba. This could be to protect his cause for writing or it could suggest the excommunication was for something trivial like copying the psalter. It seems likely that Columba was blamed for something because of the rumpus that took place at the synod, however it seems either he was not excommunicated or else he simply ignored it, because he remained in Ireland a further two years from 561 to 563. Exile preparations would have taken only a few weeks and when he did leave he was scarcely a peregrini - they travelled as far as Iceland and Italy. Columba crossed a fairly busy shipping lane to join people of his own clan. His journey was planned and was to follow up his work consolidating North Ireland by now consolidating Alban Dalriada. The legend seems to have arisen because of either propaganda or a misunderstanding of 'white martyrdom', which meant leaving your home for Christ. His cousin was King Conaill of the Dalriad Scots in Alba, who was under the power of the Pict King Brude, who in 559 had killed King Gabhran - self styled King of Alba - and was now reclaiming the Dalriad lands. The Scots were badly in need of a leader, not just a warrior, but someone who could pull them together against the Pictish threat. It is almost certain that Conaill called Columba to help him. The story of his journey is suspect; that he sailed in a coracle is probable, for some coracles could be fairly large. The legend has it that he landed on Oronsay, but could still see Ireland, so he sailed on till he and his party landed on Iona at the Port of the Coracle, looked back from Cul ri Erin, saw nothing, and so they stayed. This was the eve of Whitsun, May 12, 563 A.D.

IONA

Columba would have hugged the coast and crossed to Argyll to meet and plan with Conaill. No doubt they selected Iona, a strategic site where their ancestors were buried, and on the border between Pictland and Dalriada. It was near the Great Glen, near the shipping routes and near Dun Add the capital. It was isolated, but not too much, and was an island just right for a Celtic monastery. Only one problem. At this time it seems the Picts had taken back Iona and Mull after 559.

The cairn of the Back to Ireland is explained when it is noticed that there is a similar cairn on Colonsay (the island surely meant in the legend, for Oronsay has no hills!) and on Mull there is a cairn of the Back to Ireland and a cairn of the Back to Alba (Scotland). These in fact were boundary cairns between Pictland and Dalriada of the Scots.

The annals, Bede and Adomnan, are confusing here. It is assumed that Conaill gifted Iona to Columba, but Iona was under Pict control, so he went to Brude two years later to sort it out, and gained permission to settle from Brude. The reference to 'given the island by the Picts' may refer only to the Picts of Ardnamurchan and Morvern, who he eventually converted, or it may refer to Brude, King of the Picts, who he visited in 565. It is unlikely that he would have antagonised the Picts by settling uninvited on Iona, likewise there is no way he could have sailed round various islands 'looking back' when the Pictish fleet were about. A reference in Adomnan only says that Columba went to Britain in 563 (2 years after Culdremne). This with Bede's account suggests he spent two years obtaining Iona. Tradition has it he settled in 563, all that can be sure is that by 565 he had Pictish approval and had established Iona as a monastery.

There are two popular stories of this time which both have some bearing on reality. The first is of Oran, the second of the welcoming bishops. Both are found in the Old Irish Life. It is possible that the two monks were the hereditary remnant of the Patrician college of seven bishops sent out as missionaries but rejected by Columba either for being apostate to pagan ways or because they were hereditary, therefore not true bishops. Oran was not recorded as being a follower of Columba by Adomnan. He could have been one of the above monks or possibly even Oran of Latteragh who died in 548 and is recorded in the martyrology of Angus. His name is used of the graveyard because of his self sacrifice to consecrate the land. It is a tale mixed with pagan ideas which reflect the attitude of the Celtic Church at that time; likewise self sacrifice is not an unusual practice. The event remains a mystery.

Iona, the dove, is the latinised form of I meaning an island. The highest point is still known as Dun-I, meaning the hill of the island. The island is separated from the western tip of Mull by the Sound of Iona, a channel of difficult currents. The monastery was to become the mother church of Dalriada – it was a perfect site to worship God in nature. The machair and other areas were developed into fine land (and still are) helped by the abundance of shell sand for lime, seaweed for compost and rain. Against the monks was the wind. They brought new farming methods to Alba; till then the Britons and Picts had been pastoral. Mull wood would have been used for building and there are plenty of reeds on Mull to use for thatch. The diet was good – bread, milk, fish and eggs, with meat for guests and for feast days and Sundays. The monks ate sparingly though, unlike the warriors who gorged themselves. Fasting and austere diets were common, but not to the extent of the anchorites.

The brothers wore dark material and the Abbot wore white; both wore sandals. haircut was from the druids and not from Patrick. They observed five daily offices, except compline, and kept Saturday as the Sabbath and Sunday as the Lord's Day – a celebration with the Eucharist presided by a bishop when present or one or two presbyters. The style of worship was of Eastern influence (through St. Martin?) consisting of hymns and psalms. Since the church was small we must presume they worshipped together out of doors.

The hermit's cell is of perhaps a later date than Columba, but

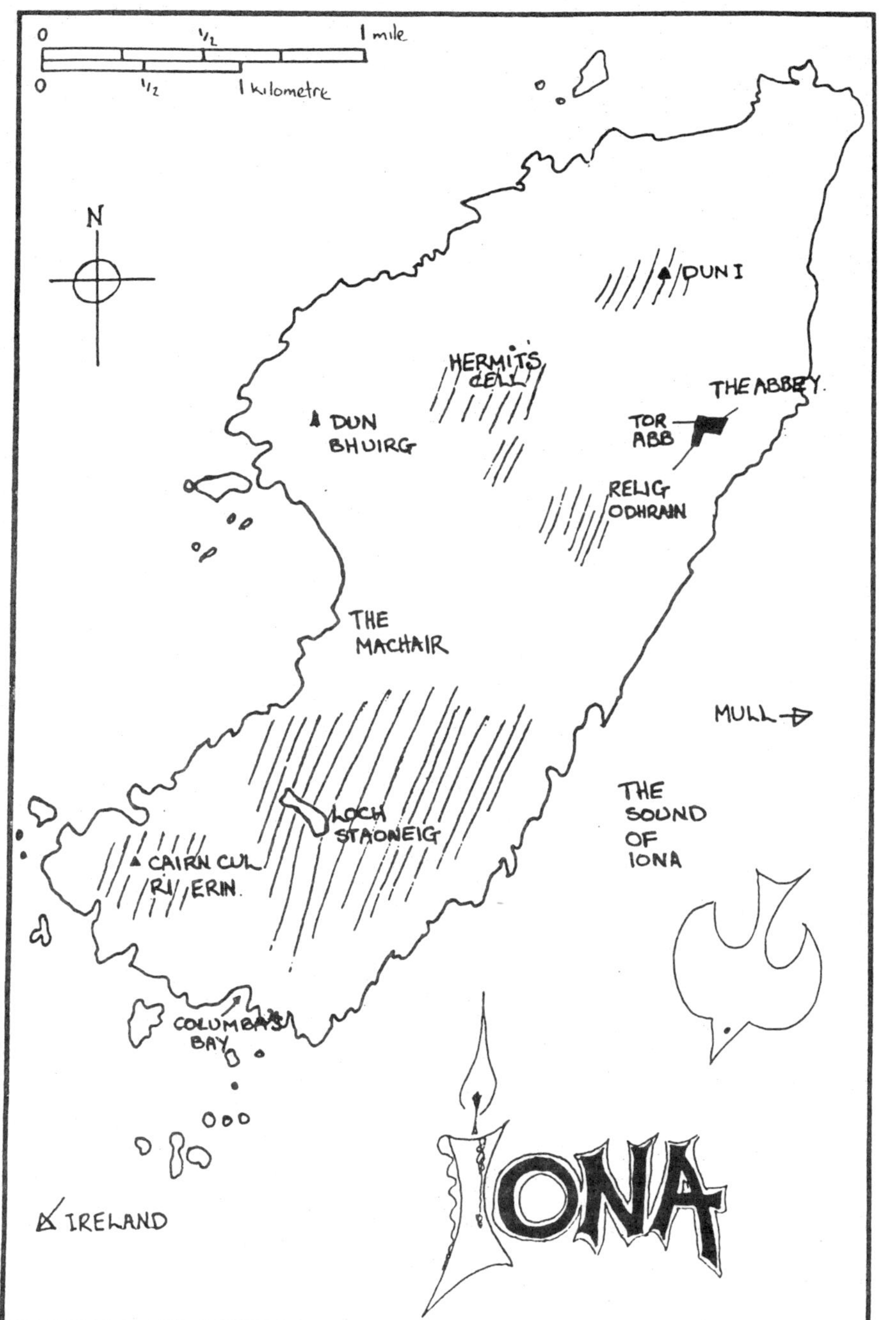

0   ½   1 mile
0   ½   1 kilometre
N
DUN I
HERMIT'S CELL
THE ABBEY
DUN BHUIRG
TOR ABB
RELIG ODHRAIN
THE MACHAIR
MULL
THE SOUND OF IONA
LOCH STAONEIG
CAIRN CUL RI ERIN
COLUMBA'S BAY
IRELAND
IONA

its site in the centre of the island reflects the monks personal battles against evil and shows an anchorite influence. Columba often spent time on his own writing, praying, reading and sorting himself out. The Iona monks differed in two ways from the anchorites; first their outward evangelical mission; and secondly their love of learning and teaching. The seniors taught and copied books; the workers farmed, fished, baked, rowed and built; and the juniors studied the psalter.

BRUDE

That Columba converted the Picts is the greatest myth, but it seems to have no bearing. In 565 he went with two monks who were Irish Picts, Comgall of Bangor and Cainnech of Achaboe, up the Great Glen to meet King Brude. Adomnan keeps their names secret in order to boost Columba's status. Brude was King of the Picts from 555 – 584. His father was Maeglwyn, a Christian King in North Wales, but Brude remained a pagan. He was over-king of the Orkneys and now Dalriada as well to an extent. Columba's aim may have been to convert Brude, but there is no evidence that this was successful. The main reason seems to have been to gain permission to settle on Iona and to make agreements with Brude, so that he would cease to harass the Dalriad Scots of Alba.

There is a record in Adomnan of Columba converting a few Pictish people through an interpreter. The conversion of Pictland was slow; Ninian had started long before, Columba helped a little and no land seems to have been granted, except possibly to Moluag, an Irish Pict and disciple of Comgall, who settled a house at Rosemarkie near Inverness.

The party's safe journey up the Great Glen suggests that they had warned the Picts of their visit. The arrival at the fort is recorded as a miracle when Columba caused the gates to be opened. Brude's advisor and foster father was Broichan, a druid.

The whole episode is rich in symbolism. The psalm singing defeated the pagan magic. Columba's prayers defeated the pagan magic. It was possibly Columba's knowledge of sailing that allowed him to leave in a storm. Columba's compassion led him to heal the ill Broichan partly because Brude ordered him to and partly to secure the release of Broichan's slave girl, who was a Scot. Perhaps he had a political motive for healing, none the less the use of a white stone (pumice?) reveals a healing more by faith than by magic. Broichan's druid power was broken. This meeting is very similar to Moses' encounter with the Pharoah's magician.

Three further tales have symbolic value. Columba raised an apostate Pict's dead but previously baptised son, and changed

leperous water into healing water. The first, a Biblical
parallel, was a sign for the Picts. The second is a sign to us
that he replaced the old ways with a living water. The third
tale,a typical tale, tells of an encounter with the Loch Ness
Monster. Above all this tale reveals the everyday challenge to
the monks from 'monsters' parallel to St. Antony. Columba's
politics and 'greater magic' gave him high esteem in the Pictish
court. He secured tenure of Iona and a treaty was made between
the Picts and Scots. Brude was no convert, but tolerated
Columba. Some say they became close friends; allies is a better
word.

AIDAN

King Conaill Comgall of Dalriada died in 574. Columba
intervened at once. Kingship was passed on to the best
candidate. Columba's favourite was Aidan against his brother
Eogan macGabran. Aidan had good royal blood. His mother was a
Briton from Stirling and he fought with the Roman party at
Ardderyd in 573. His wife was a Pict — the grand-daughter of
Brude, and his father had been King Gabran.

Columba was on Hinba (Eilean an Naoimh?) at the time on
retreat, not far from Dun Add. Here he had a vision that either
promoted his choice, was created by him to secure his unpopular
decision, or was exaggerated by later writers to support
Columba; whatever — Columba had a vision — a vision of a united
and Christian Alba, and Aidan was the first step. Dalriada was
small, but in later years it was to become the dominant nation.

In 574 Columba consecrated Aidan as King on Iona by the laying
on of hands. The first British Christian King who is by lineal
descent related to the present Queen. His prophetic warning to
Aidan was 'don't upset us — or else!' The church grew behind the
sword. Later that year at Kintyre the Comgall clan, angered by
Columba's choice, fought the Gabhran clan. Aidan won a costly
victory. Some implicate Columba, to reinforce the theory that he
was a warrior — it was Aidan who was the warrior. In 580 he
fought in Orkney; it is unclear whether he fought pirates or
Brude. In 582 he took the Isle of Man from the Ulida Irish for
a time. Around 590 he fought at Stirling with the prayerful
support of Columba, records Adomnan. The reference to Barbarians
by Adomnan, rather than the usual Gentiles to describe the
Picts, reinforces the theory that his enemy at Stirling was the
Miathi, a confederaton of perhaps Pictish rebels. Columba's
support here seems acceptable.

Around 600 he was defeated at Degsastone by Ethelfrith of
Northumbria. This was the archetypal Scotland v. England battle.
Defeated yes, but it shows how Aidan's power and support had

grown that he would take on the English.

DRUM CEATT

Despite later stories, explaining how he could return from exile with covered eyes to avoid seeing Ireland, Columba freely attended the convention of Drum Ceatt in 575 as King Aidan's advisor. It is hard to tell from Adomnan, but he suggests that Columba travelled freely in Ireland at this time.

Tradition has three reasons for coming;
1) to seek the freedom of Scanlon;
2) to get a better deal for the bards; and
3) to get independance for Alba Dalriada.

The first, a classic case of human rights, may be from a later date. The second concerned the bards' abuse of their right to free food and lodging (COINMED) and as a result the King had banished them (presumably from his own part of Ireland). Columba complained, knowing well their value to Irish culture, and obtained a compromise whereby coinmed was withdrawn and the bards were given their own land to work. It is said that the Anhra Columcille was composed by the grateful bards at this time. Although this is doubtful, Adomnan hints at bardic hymns about Columba. As a result of this decision, many bards entered the monasteries and Irish became a written language along with Latin.

The main reason for the convention was independance for Alban Dalriada. In 572 Baetan macCairell of the Ulida Irish expanded into Irish Dalriada. He tried to force the Irish Dalriadans to yield the Alban Dalriadan's fleet, which belonged to Aidan. The Scots in Alba were tolerated by the Picts, as long as they had a fleet. If Aidan gave up the fleet to save Irish Dalriada, then the Picts would crush him; if he refused, Baetan would take Irish Dalriada. To resolve this, the two Dalriad Kings, Aid macAinmire and Aidan, met at Drum Ceatt near Derry. Aid was not yet Ard Ri (Baetan macNinnedo was until 586) he was still a provincial King. Columba, concerned, perhaps put Aidan in touch with his cousin. Baetan was not there and the judge was Olave Brieve Colman macComgell. The result was strategic. Alban Dalriada was given independance – its fleet could not be surrendered. The wording of the agreement mentioned 'hostings' which presumably meant that help would still be given if asked for. Whether Aidan took independance, or Aid offered it, is unclear. Aidan had a strong kingdom and Aid had a weak one; to help Aid would have risked his strong kingdom. The result, however, started Scotland on its way to becoming a nation.

BATTLES

Some try to implicate Columba in as much bloodshed as possible. Others claim his eternal innocence. Whatever his own role in battles, tribal loyalties and celtic spirits sent men into battle on several occasions.

In 573 the decisive battle between Christianity and Pagandom was fought at Ardderyd near Carlisle. Rhydderech Hael of Strathclyde formed a compact with Aidan, Urien from Cumbria and the new King Cadwallow Lui of North Wales. Rhydderch marched under a green dragon standard as the Christian Champion against the pagan army led by the Archdruid Merlin, who had previously defeated the legendary Arthur. Rhydderch shattered the pagans.

As a result Britain was opened up to the Irish and Welsh monks, and the British monks returned home - such as Kentigern who went back to Eglais Chu, his 'beloved place', better known as Glasgow. Monks travelled as far as Orkney and Brittany. Columba's role here was as a spiritual leader in what to him must have seemed a spiritual battle. He cannot be blamed for the battle, but neither can he be excused.

In 579 the tribes of St. Comgall and St. Columba are said to have clashed at Coleraine near Derry, as a result of an argument between the two monks. This is unreliable - if such a battle took place then it is doubtful that it had anything to do with Comgall and Columba, since Adomnan records them as friends after the conference at Drum Ceatt.

In 587 it is said that the Northern and Southern Ui Neill clashed at Clonard. Colman macDiarmaid's son Cumin had killed Baodin while in the sanctuary of Columba. 5000 died. That Aid macAinmire fought for Columba suggests that the 'hostings' of Drum Ceatt were reciprocal. Whether this battle involved Columba, or whether it was sparked by tribal tension, is unknown.

As it was only Culdremne that was the supposed cause of exile, these other battles may show that Columba learned nothing from this, which reinforces the theory that the exile and penance stories were later made up to cover up the fact that Columba could involve himself in battles, certainly not as a warrior, but in a psychological and spiritual way. Besides, his praying may well have been his idea of praying for peace (compare today's churches' involvement in war and liberation struggles with this). Columba was more like Moses or one of the Old Testament Judges, and yet Adomnan records for us a man similar to a New Testament Disciple. The two are not incompatible, and the story of Columba seeing himself as glass in a friend's vision reflects his attitude to his own Celtic Iron Age habits.

Columba was an evangelist and a statesman. A tidy ascetic. His discipline of reciting the psalms lying in cold sand, show us his tougher side, but his grey eye twinkled with humour as well, for instance the tale of the cheeky boy who he told to stick out his tongue so he could touch it!

His involvement with animals, trees and water, portrays his deep Celtic heritage. The boar he cursed in Skye was symbolic of the pagan cult figure. His cursing causes problems. Was he an angry Celt; were his curses really insight; were his curses later pagan propaganda; or was cursing the only weapon he wielded?

He kept his 'second sight' a secret to avoid boasting and crowds, but his knowledge of the sea, of weather and politics, were a result of his long experience. His loud voice was both symbolic and no doubt factual. It is hard to discriminate because Adomnan plays up certain characteristics to show Columba was an apostle. He certainly tried to live an apostolic life, believing what could happen in the first century could happen also in the sixth. His retreats to Hinba deepened his understanding and God's favour on him was portrayed by the pillars of light and fireballs, so like the encounter of Paul on the Damascus road, and the angelic visitations in his cell and on the Hill of the Angel, so like the transfiguration.

He was a man who put kings in touch with each other and with God. Contrary to popular tradition he was not an exile, nor did he meddle in politics. He made politics.

Although he spent most of his time on Iona, he travelled a lot in Scotland and Ireland. He met the Picts on several occasions. He didn't convert them as a race, only a few families; but nor did he hate them – he only hated their corrupt pagan ways. There is a possibility that he knew Rhydderch Hael and even that he met St. Kentigern of Glasgow. Jocelyn's tale of their meeting is so unlike the medieval church and so vividly recorded as to suggest authenticity. No doubt they met to demark their territories. They feasted on bread and water and swapped croziers. The two groups of monks are said to have chanted "The saints shall go from strength to strength, Alleluia", and "The way of the Just is made straight", as they came together.

Columba, a man of great influence during and after his lifetime, left only a cowl, a pectoral cross, a walking stick and some books, when he died. The books, which couldn't be drowned, were much valued in the time of Adomnan.

COLUM
CILLE

HIS DEATH

Columba prophesied his own death. He wept because he had been given four more years to live before going to heaven! The account of his last days is full of detail, though some bits are obscure - like banishing snakes (there only was the common adder!). He spoke of returning the deposit of his soul to God, and of his coming sabbath. His white horse grieving him could be a pagan gloss to associate the old man with a humble old horse as a paradox on the Celtic hero and his charger. His famous prophecy about kings came true - Iona became an international burying place - and the last line referring to 'other churches' may have meant the Church of Rome.
  The apt line of psalm 34 v. 10 "those who seek the Lord lack no good thing" is typical of a Celtic monk, and he instructs Baithen, his successor, to continue "Come, O sons, listen to me . . ." (RSV)
He had put off his death at Easter to avoid spoiling the festival, and now his time had come. He blessed the community and, at midnight on the Lord's day, he rushed to the altar and died making the sign of the cross in the arms of his attendant Diarmit.

Columba died on June 9th 597 A.D. He was 76.

A three day rainless storm, which kept travellers off the island, was possible and would explain the lights in the sky mentioned in his friend's visions. All these events are based on the truth. Just not all of the truth!

HIS IMPACT

Bede wrote saying, whoever Columba was - his successors were good. Either he knew little of Columba, or perhaps what he heard was not complimentary. History has selectively passed on the story of the dove of the church, perhaps the pigeon is a more suitable name. His successors went out from Iona all over Europe relighting the candles blown out by the Goths. Rome became anxious of this 'liberated' Celtic Church. In 597 Gregory the Pope sent Augustine to revive the See of Canterbury, but it was the monks of Iona who did most of the work of evangelising the Angles.
  King Oswald of Northumbria (who had been exiled from Scotland) called Aidan the monk to come and spread his teachings to his people. Aidan chose Lindisfarne, a small island cut off by tides, as his monastery. The church spread North and South from Lindisfarne. Oswald was defeated by the pagan Penda, who was in

turn defeated by Oswald's brother Oswill, who became King. His wife was of the Roman tradition, so they celebrated Easter at different times. This had arisen because the Roman Church had revised their calendar tables while Ireland was cut off. The matter was settled at Whitby in 664, called by Oswill. Wilfred, a good public speaker, swamped the Columban Colman with the accusation that he held Columba to be greater than Peter, the patron of the Roman Church, to whom the keys had been given. There was an enforced unity of church practise thereafter. One enforcement that has caused trouble ever since. One wonders what might have happened if Colman had won the argument. Would there have been a united Britain sooner and would the slaughters of the Americas have been prevented if Celtic monks had been sent as missionaries? Colman returned to Iona where the monks stuck to their own ways. Adomnan travelled to Jarrow in 679 and was converted to the Roman ways of Easter and haircut. His return to face the angered monks may explain why he wrote such a beautiful account of Columba to show his allegiance to this Saint who was every bit an apostle! After the synod of Tara most Irish Scots went the Roman way. Only a few pockets of resistance remained – Iona among them. For a time there were two communities on Iona, the pro-Peter and the pro-Columba. By 767 Iona had adopted the Roman ways.

King Kenneth McAlpine moved the Columban Church from Iona to Dunkeld to avoid the Vikings. Many monks returned to Ireland, taking with them the uncompleted 'Book of Kells'. McAlpine was a half Pict, half Scot with wholly Scotic sympathies. His rule united the lands of Dalriada and Pictland as a decisive step towards a united Alba. The Columban Church took over the British and Pictish Churches. For instance, the monastery at Deer, Aberdeenshire, founded by Drastan, a Pict, was rededicated to Columba. (Later still it was rededicated to Peter! This was to be the eventual outcome for the whole Columban Church). This also explains why there were Irish round towers in the heart of Pictland, for instance Brechin. Candida Casa had fallen to the English, and Bangor in Ireland was cut off by the Vikings. The Columban Church predominated. Columba was the chosen Saint and apostle of Alba. Ninian and Kentigern were great monks, but Columba was a Scot. An Irish hero for his support in tribal warfare, and a Scottish saint for his consolidating the country into a Christian Kingdom.

In the 11th and 12th centuries, however, a wave of Roman influence spread through Scotland and Ireland, and reformed the monastic system, so that from 1200 there was a regular Benedictine monastery on Iona up to the Reformation. It was not destroyed by the Protestants, but slowly dissolved and had gone by the 17th century. The Celtic Church had gone. The Culdees of the 12th and 13th centuries were thought not to be Celtic, but rather the remnants of some anchorite monks.

The Benedictine Cathedral (dedicated to St. Mary) was rebuilt by the Duke of Argyll at the beginning of the 20th century. The Columban Church has gone, but its influence on Scotland and Europe has been immense. The Celts held out against the savages – the Picts and the Angles – until they were savage no more; and they saved Christendom after the fall of Rome by protecting much of its literature, training monks and spreading out as peregrini to reinvade Europe with love. It was the golden age of the Celt. Perhaps it was the only time the Celts were united! It was just in time, for soon after Islam raged throughout the world. The Columban monks inspired the Benedictines to continue the evangelism. Europe was saved for Christ.

Iona is again an important centre for sending out Christians to reawaken the people of Britain with a living Gospel. George MacLeod started the work of rebuilding the Abbey and outhouses in 1938 as a social experiment involving clergy and craftsmen. They rebuilt the Abbey and then set out to rebuild the community. It is this work that the Iona Community continues today.

The old aim of Columba is similar to our aim today to work for a true unity through the Church Militant, involved in political change and spiritual enlightenment. The statue of the incarnation is at the heart of the Abbey and it is incarnation that is at the heart of the Community's life.

Columba sought to mix the secular with the sacred, to consolidate and then evangelise. It is this same principle we use today. We give people the opportunity to rebuild their lives in our Cities and on Iona, and it is through this that they learn that God loves them. Iona is a candle burning in the darkness and the darkness has never put it out. We are still the second generation Christians. This is still the age of the miracle!

POSTSCRIPT

Which is more useful to us today – myth or fact? There is a place for stained glass and there is a place for stark realism. That we cannot simplify Columba is exciting. He and his world were as complex as ours is today. There was a place for myths in his day to try to grasp fundamental truths. There is just as much need for such myths today. A myth is no less important because it isn't factual; it is the fundamental truth that is important. The fundamental truth is, as it was to Columba and Peter before him, that 'God loves us' and God calls us to reciprocate this love by loving one another. God has shown us on the cross how much the cost is of this love. We have been shown

A broken stained-glass window
which Rev. George MacLeod had
seen was transformed from

"Glory to God in the Highest"

into

"Glory to God in the High Street"

how to live this way, and we are given the help of the Holy Spirit, which we symbolise in baptism. Jesus said "follow me".

One Easter on Iona a group of us went on Pilgrimage to St. Columba's Bay. A friend of ours had chosen to be baptised on Easter Sunday, so that he might receive his first communion at the celebration of our Lord's resurrection. He had chosen Columba's Bay because of the myth which tells that this was the place where Columba buried his coracle and "did not go back". Factually this is unlikely, but the fundamental truth is, Jesus said "follow me".

Why then is Columba not the Patron Saint of Scotland? During the 'Easter controversy' the relics of St. Andrew the apostle were landed and taken to Kilrymont in Fife (now St. Andrews). Columba was out of favour at the time, so Andrew became the Patron Saint of Scotland.

It is not such a bad deal. Andrew left a few bones. Columba left a vision. A vision of political and spiritual unity.

Jesus said "follow me!".

BIBLIOGRAPHY

Adomnan's Life of St. Columba   A.O. & M.O. Anderson 1961

Historical St. Columba   D. Simpson 1963

Columba   I. Findlay 1979

The Magnificent Gael   Reginald Hale 1975
          (original script - Iona Abbey : unpublished in UK)

A Record and a Tribute   Duncan MacGregor 1898

A Church History of Scotland   Burleigh

Oxford Dictionary of the Christian Church

Adomnan's Life of St. Columba   W Reeves 1874

Adomnan's Life of St. Columba   W. Huyshe 1905

Bede's History of the English Church and People

The Legend of St. Columba   P. Colum

The Columban Church   J. Duke 1950

The Celtic Church in Britain and Ireland   Zimmer

St. Columba   L. Menzies 1920

The Dove of the Church or Columcille   R. Thompson 1980

Iona, Its History and Archeology   R. Reece

The Life of St. Mungo (Kentigern)   A. Gits 1977

Celtic Scotland   Skene 1886
   (esp. Vol.II appendix - the Old Irish Life of St. Columba)

Early Christian Ireland   K. Hughes 1972

SONGS OF THE INCARNATION   ISBN 0 9501351 8 6
         John Bell & Graham Maule

THE IONA COMMUNITY WORSHIP BOOK   ISBN 0 9501351 9 4

THROUGH WOOD AND NAILS   Record — No. 146/REC/S,   Cassette — IC/WGP/001
A record and cassette which includes many of the songs and worship found
         in the above books, recorded in Iona Abbey

POVERTY, CHASTITY AND OBEDIENCE — A Vocation for Today
John Bell & Graham Maule   ISBN 0 947988 00 9

THE WHOLE EARTH SHALL CRY GLORY — Iona Prayers by Rev. George F. MacLeod
Paperback   ISBN 0 947988 01 7   Hardback   ISBN 0 947988 04 1

LIVING STONES — Unity Where it Matters   ISBN 0 947988 02 5
         Jim Maitland

WHAT ON EARTH IS GOD LIKE? — Three Bible Studies   ISBN 0 947988 03 3
         Jean C. Morrison

WILD GOOSE SONG BOOK   ISBN 0 947988 05 X
         John Bell & Graham Maule

WILD GOOSE PRINTS No.1   ISBN 0 947988 06 8
         John Bell & Graham Maule

WHAT IS THE IONA COMMUNITY?   ISBN 0 947988 07 6

WOMEN'S WORDS FROM IONA ABBEY   ISBN 0 947988 08 4
         Kathryn Galloway

A TOUCHING PLACE   Cassette IC/WGP/004   Book   ISBN 0 947988 09 2
         John Bell & Graham Maule

WILD GOOSE PRINTS No.2   ISBN 0 947988 10 6
         John Bell & Graham Maule

COLUMBA — The Man and the Myth   ISBN 0 947988 11 4
         Mitchell Bunting

IN PRAISE OF GOD'S GOODNESS   ISBN 0 947988 12 2
         Kathryn Galloway

THE IONA PILGRIMAGE — One Man's Experience   ISBN 0 947988 13 0
         Jack Kellet

A CHILD'S STORY   ISBN 0 947988 14 9
         Caroline Clarke

Other new publications are in preparation   —   please enquire for details